Building an Effective Prayer Life
Workbook

Antonio M. Palmer

Building an Effective Prayer Life Workbook

Copyright © 2017 by Antonio M. Palmer

ISBN 978-1-947741-06-5

All rights reserved. No part of this book may be reproduced or transmitted in any form or by any means without written permission of the author.

Unless otherwise indicated, all Scripture quotations are taken from the New King James Version, copyright © 1979, 1980, 1982 by Thomas Nelson, Inc. Publishers. Scripture quotations noted KJV are from the King James Version. Scripture quotations noted NIV are from the Holy Bible: New International Version® Copyright © 1973, 1978, 1984 by International Bible Society. Used by permission of Zondervan Publishing House. All rights reserved. Scripture quotations noted NLT are from the Holy Bible, New Living Translation, copyright © 1996. Used by permission of Tyndale House Publishers, Inc. Wheaton, Illinois 60189. All rights reserved. Scripture quotations noted NASB are from the New American Standard Bible ®, copyright © the Lockman Foundation 1960, 1962, 1963, 1968, 1971, 1972, 1973, 1975, 1977. Used by permission. Scripture quotations noted AMPLIFIED or AMP are taken from the Amplified ® Bible, copyright © 1954, 1958, 1962, 1964, 1965, 1987 by the Lockman Foundation. Used by permission (www.Lockman.org). Scripture quotations noted The Complete Jewish Bible are taken from The Complete Jewish Bible, copyright © 1998 by David H. Stern. Published by Jewish New Testament Publication, Inc. www.messianicjewish.net/jntp. Distributed by Messianic Jewish Resources. www.messianicjewish.net. All rights reserved. Used by permission. Scripture quotations noted The Message Bible are from The Message Bible. Copyright © 1993, 1994, 1995, 1996, 2000, 2001, 2002. Used by permission of NavPress Publishing Group

Published by Kingdom Publishing, LLC

1350 Blair Drive, Odenton, MD 21113

Printed in the USA

TABLE OF CONTENTS

Chapter One
What is Prayer?
1

Chapter Two
Three Key Benefits of Prayer
5

Chapter Three
Acceptable Prayer
11

Chapter Four
Why We Need to Pray
13

Chapter Five
Why We Don't Pray
17

Chapter Six
Hindrances to Answered Prayers
19

Chapter Seven
The Model Prayer of Jesus
23

Chapter Eight
Effective Praying
29

Chapter Nine
Praying in the Holy Ghost
43

Building Your Prayer Life
Let's Begin to Pray!
49

Chapter One

What is Prayer?

> **KEY SCRIPTURE**
>
> "If My people who are called by My name will humble themselves, and *pray* and seek My face, and turn from their wicked ways, then I will hear from heaven, and will forgive their sin and heal their land." (2 Chronicles 7:14)

From the above scripture, what are the four things that the Lord desires for His people to do in order for Him to respond in a favorable way for them?

1. _____
2. _____
3. _____
4. _____

What are the three things that the Lord promises to do in response to our penitent actions of 2 Chronicles 7:14?

1. _____
2. _____
3. _____

In your own words, what does prayer mean to you?

_____
_____

DEFINITION OF PRAYER

Miriam-Webster's Dictionary defines prayer as
_____
_____

The British Dictionary (cited on www.dictionary.com) defines prayer as
_____
_____
_____

The Easton's Bible Dictionary says that prayer is
_____; the _____ of the soul with God; not in contemplation or meditation, but in direct address to Him. It is _____ the Lord (Exodus 32:11), _____ _____ the soul before the Lord (1 Samuel 1:15), and _____ _____ to God (Psalm 73:28).

We first see this dialogue between man and God in Genesis 3:8, "And they heard the voice of the Lord walking in the cool of the day..." and after Adam hid himself from God because of his disobedience, God calls for the man, "Adam, where art thou?" Prayer is a two-way conversation with God. It is communion with Him which involves intimate communication.

After the fall of Man, we see prayer enacted in Genesis 4:26, "And as for Seth, to him also a son was born; and he named him Enosh. Then *men began to call on the name of the Lord.*"

BIBLICAL WORDS FOR PRAYER

In the New Testament there are several Greek words that are translated as prayer such as *deomai, eratao, euchomai, parakaleo, proseuche (proseuchomai)* and *aiteo*. Let's define each word:

1. Deomai means _____

2. Eratao means _____

3. Euchomai means _____

4. Parakaleo means _____

5. Proseuche means _____

  (Proseuchomai is a derivative of proseuche which simply means to offer prayers)

6. Aiteo means _____

From these New Testament words for prayer we can conclude that prayer means "to beseech, ask, beg, entreat, call to one's side, address, speak to, call upon or make a request." Also, from these New Testament words we can say that prayer is often produced from a heart that craves for, longs for, or desires God and His will to be done and for needs to be fulfilled. You will rarely pray for something you do not desire.

The key word for prayer is _____.

Beseech means

_____

_____

Beseeching prayer is an earnest plea. It is sincere, deep and intense – just like God wants it. Prayer is intense. God isn't into dull moments or dull relationships and you shouldn't be either. He is looking for intimate conversations from people who are passionate toward Him.

Chapter Two
Three Key Benefits of Prayer

Dr. David Yonggi Cho, pastor of the largest church in the world, said in his book, Prayer that Brings Revival, "God has created us in such a way that we need to know the purpose and benefit of something if we are going to be motivated to work for that thing. If we actually knew the benefits of prayer, we would have been praying by now. Motivation works on the basis of desire. For someone to pray, he must learn to desire prayer. How can you develop the desire to pray? You must see the eternal and temporal benefits of prayer."

He goes on to talk about three unique benefits of prayer. I'd like to briefly discuss these three benefits hoping that it will spark a desire in you to pray. The three benefits that Dr. Cho shares in his book are

1. _____
2. _____
3. _____

PRAYER PRODUCES POWER

To develop power in prayer we must change our _____ about prayer. In the gospel according to Matthew, Jesus made a revolutionary statement regarding the attitude necessary to produce spiritual power.

> ## MATTHEW 11:11-12
> "Verily I say unto you, among them that are born of women there hath not risen a greater than John the Baptist; notwithstanding he that is least in the kingdom of heaven is greater than he. And from the days of John the Baptist until now the kingdom of heaven suffereth violence, and the violent take it by force"

The attitude that Jesus states here for prayer is an attitude of _____.

Adam Clarke called the violence that Jesus referred to as the "_____."

Violence means _____.

The violent are those who, like a hurricane, will destroy anything in their path that will interrupt or hinder their sincere devotion to God. IT WILL TAKE A VIOLENT DEDICATION TO PRAYER TO BRING THE POWER OF GOD INTO OUR LIVES. This violent earnestness or dedication will be most evident in our _____. Power in prayer takes much time. For this reason we must ___ _____ for our time.

Corrie ten Boom said, "Don't pray when you feel like it. _____
_____.
A man is powerful on his knees."

Revivalist John Wesley says, "God does nothing except in response to _____ _____." In fact, if we never pray, God is not obligated to do anything for us. When we pray, God cannot deny Himself.

The very reason why there were so many miracles in the ministry of Jesus and in the early church is because of prayer. The reason why there is little or limited power in today's church is simply because of the lack of prayer. I like what Archbishop Nicholas Duncan-Williams say about the church's lack of prayer. He calls it an epidemic which he labeled as the PWC virus – Prayerlessness without Ceasing. We must pray with violent earnestness if we are going to seize the kingdom of heaven and release God's power.

Prayer produces power and we should be motivated by the fact that God desires to use us to demonstrate His awesome power. However, He only demonstrates His power in answer to believing prayer. His power should give you a desire to pray.

S. D. Gordon gave an awesome quote about prayer. He said, "The great people of the earth today are the people who pray! I do not mean those who talk about prayer; or those who say they believe in prayer; or those who explain prayer; but I mean those who _____ ____ __ ____. They have not time. It must be taken from something else. That something else is important, very important and pressing, but still, less important and pressing than prayer. There are people who put prayer first, and group the other items in life's schedule around and after prayer. These are the people today who are doing the most for God in winning souls, in solving problems, in awakening churches, in supplying both men and money for mission posts, in keeping fresh and strong their lives far off in sacrificial service on the foreign field, where the thickest fighting is going on, and in keeping the old earth sweet a little while longer."

E. M. Bounds made the great statement, "Real prayer is not learned in a classroom but in the _____."

If you're reading this book, you my friend, have the awesome privilege to begin a life of prayer that can produce the kind of power that will shape tomorrow's world.

PRAYER BRINGS BROKENNESS

God cannot fully use a person who is not _____ and completely _____ to Him. If there is anyone who knows something about brokenness it is the apostle Peter. He first encounters Jesus in the dawn of an unsuccessful fishing trip. With a boat full of empty nets and ice coolers, the rugged fisherman was overly frustrated and probably verbalizing his frustrations with vulgar outbursts. After all, he was known as a "curser." Jesus comes early in the morning while Peter was basically washing his nets, perhaps gathering his work gear and calling it a day. He makes one request of Peter to get back in the boat and let down his net one more time. When Peter finally agreed to do so, his net and his coworkers' nets caught so many fish that their nets began to tear. It was only when Peter realized what had happened that he fell to his knees before Jesus and said, "Oh, Lord, please leave me – I'm such a sinful man." He was broken by the evidence of God's power and love for him.

Brokenness is accomplished through prayer. Prayer is all about encountering God. Usually, when you come into contact with God in your prayer time, the first thing you feel in your heart as you enter into His presence is a realization of your sin – like Peter. Then you begin to confess your sin and humble yourself before Him. Abiding in His presence will produce brokenness and submission. Brokenness gives us a humbling awareness of our own _____ as sinners and of our own insignificance as powerless creatures before an omnipotent God. This ultimately leads us to an unhesitating submission to the divine will of God.

There isn't anything God desires more than to find a person with a broken heart who He can restore and use mightily. Your pain, your grief and your trials were meant to bring you closer to God. He is so _____ to us when we respond in total surrender to Him.

"The Lord is near to those who have a broken heart and saves such as have a contrite spirit" (Psalm 34:18).

Brokenness not only causes surrender to God but also a _____ upon Him. For God to do something mighty in and through us, it is going to take a dependence upon Him. We must rely on the character, power and great name of our God. He has a great track record of helping His people. Knowing that God greatly uses people who are broken, surrendered and dependent upon Him, we should have a burning desire to pray.

PRAYER GIVES US AUTHORITY
TO OVERCOME SATAN AND EVIL

Samuel Chadwick says, "The one concern of the devil is to keep Christians from praying. He fears nothing from prayerless studies, prayerless work and prayerless religion. He laughs at our toil, mocks at our wisdom, but he _____ when we pray."

William Cowper quotes, "Satan trembles when he sees ____ _____ Christian on his knees."

Chapter Three
Acceptable Prayer

"I would rather teach one man to pray than ten men to preach." Charles Spurgeon

All so often when new converts come to Christ they are encouraged to pray. That encouragement is no more than someone telling them to pray or come to a scheduled prayer meeting at the church. Simply put, they were _____ to pray and not _____ to pray. Both Jesus and John the Baptist taught their disciples how to pray (Luke 11:1). Prayer is _____.

To begin developing an effective prayer life, you would want to know what kinds of prayers are acceptable to God. There are specific things in Scripture that reveal to us what must be woven into the fabric of our prayers to God. Here are nine key components that make prayer acceptable to God:

1. Acceptable prayer must be _____ (Matthew 21:22).
2. Acceptable prayer must be _____ (Hebrews 10:22).
3. Acceptable prayer must be _____ (James 4:3).
4. Acceptable prayer must be _____ (John 15:16; 16:23-24; Ephesians 5:20; Colossians 3:17).
5. We should not pray _____ (Matthew 6:5).
   a. Hypocrites love praying standing in the synagogues
   b. Hypocrites love being seen of men

c. Hypocrites used vain repetition and much speaking

6. Acceptable prayer is _____ (James 5:16).

7. Acceptable prayer is _____ (Matthew 6:14-15).

8. Acceptable prayer is _____ (Luke 18:1).

9. Acceptable prayer is _____ (1 John 5:14).

Chapter Four
Why We Need to Pray

Where the church is advancing around the world, people are praying.

> PHILIPPIANS 4:6
>
> "Be anxious for nothing, but in everything by prayer and supplication with thanksgiving let your requests be made known to God."

One of the biggest questions that some people would ask concerning prayer is "Why pray?" They may say, "What is the point of praying when God knows the future and is already in control of everything? If we cannot change His mind, why should we pray?"

Remember the very definition of prayer involves _____ communion and conversation with God. When we pray we are inviting God into our lives. He desires unhindered, unbroken fellowship with us. Prayer does not change God's mind insomuch as it changes ____ _____.

1. Prayer is a form of _____ God (Luke 2:36-38) and _____ Him.
2. We pray because God _____ us to pray (Luke 18:1; Philippians 4:6-7; 1 Thessalonians 5:17).
3. Prayer is exemplified for us by _____ and the early church (Mark 1:35; Acts 1:14; 2:42; 3:1; 4:23-31; 6:4; 13:1-3). Think about it – if Jesus thought it was

worthwhile to pray, we should also. If He needed to pray to remain in the Father's will, how much more do we need to pray?

4. Another reason to pray is that God intends prayer to be _____ _____

    A. We pray in preparation for major decisions (Luke 6:12-13).

    B. We pray to overcome demonic barriers (Matthew 17:14-21).

    C. We prayer to gather workers for the spiritual harvest (Luke 10:2).

    D. We pray to gain strength to overcome temptation (Matthew 26:41) and

    E. We pray to obtain the means of strengthening others spiritually (Ephesians 6:18-19).

5. We have God's promise that our prayers are not in _____ even if we do not receive specifically what we ask for (Matthew 6:6; Romans 8:26, 27).

    A. He has promised that when we ask for things that are in accordance to His will, He will give us what we ask for (1 John 5:14-15).

    B. Sometimes He delays His answers according to His wisdom and for our benefit. In these situations, we are to be diligent and persistent in prayer (Matthew 7:7; Luke 18:1-8).

    C. Prayer should not be seen as our means of getting God to do our will on earth, but rather as a means of getting God's will done on earth.

    D. For situations in which we do not know God's will specifically, prayer is a means of discerning His will.

6. A lack of prayer demonstrates a lack of _____ and a lack of trust in God's word. We pray to demonstrate our faith in God, which He will do as He has promised in His word and bless our lives abundantly more than we could ask or imagine (Ephesians 3:20).

7. When righteous people pray they can _____ _____ (James 5:16).

8. Through prayer, we _____ ourselves with the Spirit (Romans 8:25-26).

9. Through prayer, we _____ to the lordship of Christ.

10. Through prayer, we learn to recognize the _____ of the Shepherd.

11. We pray to receive mercy and grace to help us in _____. (Hebrews 4:16).

12. We pray to _____ on God and not our circumstances (Psalm 77:1-12; Philippians 4:6).

Chapter Five
Why We Don't Pray

"We have not, because we ask not." James 4:1

---
1 SAMUEL 12:23

"God forbid that I should sin against the Lord in ceasing to pray for you."

There are several reasons why we do not pray. Here are some:

1. Some people don't look at it as _____ when we do not pray.

2. Some people feel _____ to pray.

3. Some people feel _____ – they are just too busy.

4. Some people simply _____

5. Some people feel _____
_____

6. Some people feel that _____

7. Some people may feel _____

8. Some people feel that _____
_____

9. Some people _____

10. Some people feel _____

11. Some people don't pray because they simply _____

12. Some people don't pray because _____

(as though they are content with life and don't want to disturb God with menial stuff).

13. Some people don't pray because _____

Write down some of the reasons why you may not pray or pray consistently:

_____
_____
_____
_____
_____

Chapter Six
Hindrances to Answered Prayers

> ### JAMES 4:1-3
>
> "What is the source of quarrels and conflicts among you? Is not the source your pleasures that wage war in your members? You lust and do not have; so you commit murder. You are envious and cannot obtain; so you fight and quarrel. You do not have because you do not ask. *You ask and do not receive, because you ask with wrong motives,* so that you may spend it on your pleasures."

When asked how much time he spent in prayer, George Muller's reply was, "Hours every day. But I live in the spirit of prayer, I pray as I walk and when I lie down and when I arise. And *the answers are always coming.*"

Our God is a prayer answering God. He says emphatically, "Call unto me and I will answer thee, and shew thee great and mighty things, which thou knowest not" (Jeremiah 33:3). When we pray God promises to respond to us. Elijah had known Him to answer by fire, "Then the fire of the Lord fell and consumed the burnt offering and the wood and the stones and the dust, and licked up the water that was in the trench" (1 Kings 18:38 NASB). Aaron and Moses, David and Solomon each experienced God answering by fire as He consumed their sacrificial offerings dedicated to Him. He will answer you when you call upon Him in faith. In Psalm 92:14-15 God explicitly says that He will deliver those who love Him, set them on high and whenever they "call upon Me and I will answer" (Psalm 92:14, 15).

Although our God desires so much to answer our prayers there are a couple of things that hinder us from receiving answers to prayers. They are:

1. _____. James 4:3 says that we ask and receive not because we ask _____, that we may spend it in our pleasures. What does it mean to "ask amiss?"

2. _____. Isaiah 59:1, 2 says that the Lord's hand is not shortened that it cannot save or His ear heavy that it cannot hear, but our iniquities have separated us from God and our sins have hid His face from us that "He will not hear."

3. _____. 1 John 3:20-22 says "if our hearts know something against us, God is greater than our hearts and He knows everything…if or hearts know nothing against us, we have confidence in approaching God; then whatever we ask for we receive from Him."

4. _____. In Ezekiel 14:3, God asks the prophet a serious question, "Son of man, these men have taken their idols into their heart…should I be inquired of (called upon or prayed to) at all by them?" Idolatry is a serious offense to God. He warned His people that He was a jealous God and that He did not want them to serve any other gods beside Him.

5. _____. God has a special love for those who are poor and the Bible even tells us that His eye is upon them insomuch that their poverty draws His special attention. In fact, the first reason why Jesus said that the Spirit of the Lord anointed Him for was to preach the gospel to the poor.

In Proverbs 21:13 God's heart toward the poor is revealed, "Whoso stoppeth his ear at the cry of the poor, he also shall cry himself, but shall not be heard." God blesses those who care for the poor and needy but He won't even entertain the prayers of those who ignore their concerns and needs.

6. _____. Mark 11:25 declares, "And when ye stand praying, forgive, if ye have ought against any; that your father also which is in heaven may forgive you your trespasses." An unforgiving spirit is one of the most subtle but most common hindrances to prayer. Our very first prayer that God answered was one of repentance where God forgave us of all our wrongdoings that we committed against Him and others. In return, He made it a requirement for us to stand forgiving others if we are to commune with Him. Anyone who is nursing a grudge against another has closed the ear of God against his own petition.

7. _____. A wrong relation between husband and wife is a hindrance to prayer. "Ye husbands, in like manner, dwell with your wives according to knowledge, giving honor unto the woman, as the weaker vessel as being also joint-heirs of the grace of life; to the end that your prayers be not hindered" (1 Peter 3:7).

8. _____. The final hindrance to prayer is found in James 1:5-7. It says, "But if any of you lacketh wisdom, let him ask of God, who giveth to all liberally and upbraideth not; and it shall be given him. But let him ask in faith, nothing doubting: for he that doubteth is like the surge of the sea driven by the wind and tossed. For let not that man think that he shall receive anything of the Lord."

Chapter Seven
The Model Prayer of Jesus

Since Jesus taught His disciples how to pray, and because prayer is teachable, we will visit "The Lord's Prayer" as our starting point for building a life of prayer (this was Jesus' disciples' starting point as well). When I first began to pray I learned and recited the Lord's Prayer. Once I understood why Jesus prayed these certain prayer points, it assisted me in building my own conversation with the Father using this prayer as my foundation. The Lord's Prayer (or The Model Prayer) is found in Matthew 6:9-13:

MATTHEW 6:9-13

"After this manner therefore pray ye: our father which art in heaven, hallowed be thy name. Thy kingdom come. Thy will be done in earth, as it is in heaven. Give us this day our daily bread. And forgive us our debts, as we forgive our debtors. And lead us not into temptation, but deliver us from evil. For thine is the kingdom, and the power, and the glory, forever. Amen."

In this model prayer Jesus makes eight essential points which I will briefly discuss. These eight prayer points are:

1. _____
2. _____
3. _____
4. _____

5. _____
6. _____
7. _____
8. _____

In this section, discuss each prayer point that Jesus prayed when He taught His disciples how to pray:

JESUS' FIRST PRAYER POINT
"OUR FATHER"

_____
_____
_____
_____
_____

JESUS' SECOND PRAYER POINT
"HALLOWED BE THY NAME"

_____
_____
_____
_____
_____

JESUS' THIRD PRAYER POINT
"THY KINGDOM COME"

_____

_____

_____

_____

JESUS' FOURTH PRAYER POINT
"THY WILL BE DONE"

_____

_____

_____

_____

JESUS' FIFTH PRAYER POINT
"OUR DAILY BREAD"

_____

_____

_____

JESUS' SIXTH PRAYER POINT
FORGIVENESS

When we pray this prayer of forgiveness there are two things you want to do:

1. Specifically name the sin that you want God to forgive you of.
2. Specifically name the people who hurt you that you are releasing from their indebtedness to you.

JESUS' SEVENTH PRAYER POINT
"DELIVERANCE FROM TEMPTATION"

JESUS' EIGHTH PRAYER POINT
"THINE IS"

Chapter Eight
Effective Praying

> "As is the business of tailors to make clothes and cobblers to make shoes, so it is the business of Christians to pray."
> Martin Luther

It is one thing to pray, but it's another thing to pray effectively. When I say "effective praying" I am talking about producing results. One thing I encourage believers to do is to make a prayer list with specific, targeted requests (the last chapter of this workbook will teach you how to build your prayer from the Lord's Prayer). The apostle Paul says, "Make your request known" (Philippians 4:6). Be specific when you petition God. DON'T PRAY AIMLESS PRAYERS. Don't just make up stuff because someone told you that you have to pray for an hour. Be specific and intentional with your words when you pray. Communicate with the Father candidly and honestly. We can come to His throne of grace "boldly." This basically means that we can be open, honest and upfront with our request. He promised that we will receive "mercy and grace to help us in the time of need" (Hebrew 4:16).

In this chapter, I will identify and highlight eight key scriptures that will help you become an effective-praying believer.

THE EFFECTUAL FERVENT PRAYERS OF THE RIGHTEOUS

> ### JAMES 5:16-18
> "Confess your faults one to another, and pray one for another, that ye may be healed. The effectual fervent prayer of a righteous man availeth much. Elias was a man subject to like passions as we are, and he prayed earnestly that it might not rain: and it rained not on the earth by the space of three years and six months. And he prayed again, and the heaven gave rain, and the earth brought forth her fruit."

1. According to James 5:16, who should we confess our faults (sins) to?
   _____

2. Can you name some inward things that we need healing from?
   _____
   _____

3. We do not get rid of sins by covering them but _____ them.

"He who conceals his sins does not prosper, but whoever confesses and renounces them finds mercy" (Proverbs 28:13).

The apostle James says that the kind of prayer of a righteous man that avails much is _____ and _____.

What does it mean to pray "effectually and fervently?"
_____
_____

_____

_____

_____

> **THE KIND OF PRAYER THAT CAN PRODUCE RESULTS IS AN ACTIVE, PASSIONATE CONVERSATION THAT A RIGHTEOUS PERSON HAS WITH GOD.**

Another key element in this equation is that James says the person must be _____. Simply put, righteousness is right standing with God. In order to be in right standing with God, you must be born again through faith in the redeeming blood of Jesus Christ. Afterwards, you yield your life to the Lordship of Christ in purity of heart and a lifestyle change that follows sound biblical principles. Righteousness can position you to be able to pray effectively.

James gives us an example of a righteous man who prayed fervently and produced results. This man was the prophet Elijah. Why do you feel the Apostle James cited Elijah as an example of a righteous man who prayed?

_____

_____

_____

_____

_____

_____

The Apostle James says that Elijah prayed "earnestly." What do you think he meant by "earnest?"

_____

_____

CLEAN CONSCIENCE (HEART)

> ### 1 JOHN 3:20-22
> "For if our heart condemn us, God is greater than our heart, and knoweth all things. Beloved, if our heart condemn us not, then have we confidence toward God. And whatsoever we ask, we receive of him, because we keep his commandments, and do those things that are pleasing in his sight."

What does the Apostle John mean when he says, "our heart condemns us?"

_____

_____

_____

_____

How is God "greater than our heart?"

_____

_____

_____

How can we gain confidence toward God?

_____

_____

_____

What happens when we have confidence toward God?

_____

_____

PRAYING HIS WILL

> **1 JOHN 5:14-15**
>
> "And this is the confidence that we have in Him, that, if we ask anything according to His will, He heareth us: and if we know that He hears us, whatsoever we ask, we know that we have the petitions that we desired of Him."

The Apostle John reveals another key element to praying effectively is praying His will. Simply put, God's will is His purpose, plans and desires. GOD'S WILL IS WHAT'S ON HIS HEART. It's what He is interested in.

What happens when we ask (pray) according to His will?

_____

_____

_____

What's the result of praying according to His will?

_____

_____

ABIDING IN CHRIST

> **JOHN 15:7-8**
>
> "If ye abide in me, and my words abide in you, ye shall ask what ye will, and it shall be done unto you. Herein is my Father glorified, that ye bear much fruit; so shall ye be my disciples."

Charles H. Spurgeon wrote, "If you want that splendid power in prayer, you must remain in loving, living, lasting, conscious, practical, abiding union with the Lord Jesus Christ."

What does it mean to "abide" in Christ?

_____

_____

_____

What is Christ's promise to us if we abide in Him?

_____

_____

_____

Smith Wigglesworth, a mighty evangelist and revivalist who had great miracles demonstrated in his ministry, testified of his prayer life. He said that he seldom prayed for more than thirty minutes but never went thirty minutes without praying. Now that's abiding in Christ. That is effective praying.

The Prophet Daniel is an example of a man who abode in prayer. According to Daniel 6:10, how many times did Daniel pray each day? _____

What did Daniel do when the political leaders of his day sent out a decree for no one to petition God for thirty days? _____

What was the result of Daniel continuing in prayer in the face of danger?
_____
_____
_____
_____

PERSISTENCE IN PRAYER

> ### LUKE 18:1-8
>
> "And He spake a parable unto them to this end, that men ought always to pray, and not to faint; saying, there was in a city a judge, which feared not God, neither regarded man: and there was a widow in that city; and she came unto him, saying, avenge me of mine adversary. And he would not for a while: but afterward he said within himself, though I fear not God, nor regard man; yet because this widow troubleth me, I will avenge her, lest by her continual coming she weary me. And the Lord said, hear what the unjust judge saith. And shall not God avenge his own elect, which cry day and night unto him, though He bear long with them? I tell you that He will avenge them speedily. Nevertheless when the Son of man cometh, shall he find faith on the earth?"

Jesus was frequently concerned that His followers pray continually in order to accomplish the will of the Father for their lives. The main point of Jesus' parable is that for prayer to be effective we must be persistent. We learn several things about effective praying from this parable:

1. Men ought _____ to pray.

2. Men should not _____ in praying.

3. Recognize what is _____ yours.

4. Understand you have an _____.

5. Cause _____ when you pray.

6. Know that Jesus sees persistence in prayer as _____.

THE PRAYER OF AGREEMENT

> **MATTHEW 18:18-20**
> "Verily I say unto you, whatsoever ye shall bind on earth shall be bound in heaven: and whatsoever ye shall loose on earth shall be loosed in heaven. Again I say unto you, that if two of you shall agree on earth as touching any thing that they shall ask, it shall be done for them of my Father which is in heaven. For where two or three are gathered together in my name, there am I in the midst of them."

We have such an awesome power when we can come together in agreement. This is why Satan fights unity so hard. He knows that once we start agreeing on earth, the Father shall bring to pass what we ask for. There are four ingredients that must be enacted in our prayer of agreement in order for the Father to materialize it on our behalf. These four ingredients include:

1. Ingredient #1 - _____. To bind (Gk. Deo) means to put under an obligated commitment and to loose (Gk. Luo) means to free from an obligated commitment. We must put ourselves under an obligated commitment if we are going to be effective in praying with one another. We are obligated to uphold our end of the bargain. This is similar to a business contract where we must be responsible for doing everything that we said we would do in the framework of our agreement.

2. Ingredient #2 - _____. To agree means to be LIKEMINDED and SUPPORTIVE. We must find someone of like mind that wants to ask God for something you both believe is the will of God for your lives.

The Prophet Amos denotes, "How can two walk together except they be agreed?" (Amos 3:3)

3. Ingredient #3 _____. The word "thing" here is pragma which means concerning what is to be accomplished; business, matters, or affairs. To touch any *thing* means to settle or resolve what you are willing to accomplish together.

4. Ingredient #4 _____. Once you know what thing you ought to accomplish together you must ask God for it together. There's a little bit deeper meaning to this as well. The literal Greek word that Jesus uses here for ask is *aiteo* which not only means to request but also to desire or crave for. I believe that when we request something from God together we also should passionately desire for it to come to pass together. Find someone that will be just as passionate about the very thing that you want to see God materialize in your life and pray consistently together with them until you see it come to pass.

THE EFFECTIVE PRAYER FORMULA

> ### MARK 11:22-24
> "And Jesus answering saith unto them, have faith in God. For verily I say unto you, that whosoever shall say unto this mountain, be thou removed, and be thou cast into the sea; and shall not doubt in his heart, but shall believe that those things which he saith shall come to pass; he shall have whatsoever he saith. Therefore I say unto you, what things soever ye desire, when ye pray, believe that ye receive them, and ye shall have them."

This passage of Scripture is a key element to effective prayer. It reveals the posture your faith must take once you decide to verbalize aloud what you want God to do for you. You must:

1. _____. This means to trust the Father wholeheartedly. The Lord never turns away a person who depends upon His name, His character and His power. "Trust in the Lord with all thine heart; and lean not unto thine own understanding. In all thy ways acknowledge Him, and He shall direct thy paths" (Proverbs 3:5, 6). When we call upon Him, we must believe that He is (Hebrew 11:6). He is trustworthy. He is all-powerful. He is a loving God. He is able to do exceedingly abundantly above all we ask or think (Ephesians 2:20).

2. _____. God requires for us to open up our mouths and say exactly what it is that we want or need from Him. He moves upon what we say. He himself brought the world into existence by what He said. There is creative power in speaking words. When we speak words of faith to Him, He goes into creative mode and creates exactly what we need manifested in our lives. We shall have what we say.

3. _____. This is a vital and pivotal part of this formula. Doubt can be a major hindrance to answered prayers. The NT Greek word used here for doubt is *diakrino* which means "to separate or to withdraw oneself from; to oppose." When we say or release our prayers to the Father, we must be careful not to sever ourselves from it by using words and actions that are in contrast to what we said. Be careful what you say after you pray. Don't walk away from what you say! Keep saying what you originally said until it comes to pass.

4. _____. Psalm 37:4 tells us that the Father "shall give thee the desires of thine hearts." This comes after we "delight ourselves in the Lord." There are two things to consider here:

    a. _____

    b. _____

5. _____.

Jesus promises that the result from using this effective prayer formula is "ye shall have them." When you take this posture as you pray God will surely manifest tangible results on your behalf.

PRAYING WITH THANKSGIVING

COLOSSIANS 4:2
"Continue in prayer, and watch in the same with thanksgiving."

As mentioned earlier, In order for our prayers to be effective we must be persistent in prayer. Here, in Colossians 4:2, his is reiterated, "Continue (be steadfast) in prayer." But this time the Apostle Paul adds another element. As we are in constant prayer we must do it with "thanksgiving." I believe the reason for thanksgiving is to keep us in the right attitude and apprecitive of the things that God does for us. "In everything give thanks: for this is the will of God in Christ Jesus concerning you" (1 Thessalonians 5:18). Giving thanks in everything is God's will for us. Other Scripture verses that point out that we should be thankful as we pray are:

"Be careful for nothing; but in everything by prayer and supplication with thanksgiving let your requests be made known unto God" (Philippians 4:6), "And whatsoever ye do in word or deed, do all in the name of the Lord Jesus, giving thanks to God and the Father by Him" (Colossians 3:17), and "I exhort therefore, that, first of all, supplications, prayers, intercessions, and giving of thanks, be made for all men" (1 Timothy 2:2).

Take a moment to list some things that you are thankful to God for. This will help you keep a good attitude and perspective in your prayer life.

_____
_____
_____
_____
_____
_____
_____
_____
_____
_____
_____
_____
_____

Chapter Nine
Praying in the Holy Ghost

> "But ye, beloved, build up yourselves on your most holy faith,
> *praying always in the Holy Ghost.*"
> (Jude 1:20)

Praying in the Holy Ghost is synonymous with praying in the Spirit. When we pray in the Spirit it involves praying with one's _____ (1 Corinthians 14:15).

Your spirit is that part of you that is created in the likeness of God. Jesus says, "God is a Spirit: and they that worship Him must worship Him in spirit and in truth" (John 4:24). Our spirit man can worship and he can pray.

In the above mentioned Scripture, the Apostle Jude gracefully challenges us to build up our most holy faith. There are several ways that we can build up or strengthen ourselves in the faith. List some of those ways:

1. _____
2. _____
3. _____
4. _____
5. _____
6. _____

How did the Apostle Jude instruct us to build up our most holy faith?

_____

The Apostle Paul mentions "praying in the Spirit" to the church of Ephesus, "Praying always with all prayer and supplication in the Spirit" (Ephesians 6:18).

The Apostle Paul also teaches this powerful truth to the church of Corinth. He says,

---

1 CORINTHIANS 14:2

"For he that speaketh in an unknown tongue speaketh not unto men, but unto God: for no man understandeth him; howbeit in the Spirit he speaketh mysteries."

There are three specific truths Paul reveals to us in this verse:

1._____
_____

2._____
_____

3._____
_____

The Apostle Paul later tells the church of Corinth that when he prays in tongues his spirit is praying but his mind is unfruitful (without understanding). He says, "I will pray with the spirit and I will pray with the mind also" (1 Corinthians 14:14, 15). Thus, when we pray in tongues or in the Spirit, our spirit man is praying.

When we are praying in the Spirit our mind is _____. You are not going to know what you are saying to God. Not having knowledge of something always make it difficult for us humans. The unknown always take a deeper dimension of faith and trust in God.

There are just some things that you will not figure out with your own finite intellect. This is where faith and trust in God has to kick in. For example:

His love surpasses our _____ (Ephesians 3:19)

His peace surpasses our _____ (Philippians 47)

His judgments are _____ and

His ways are _____ (Romans 11:33).

Jesus comforted the disciples by saying,

> ### LUKE 11:11-13
> "If a son shall ask bread of any of you that is a father, will he give him a stone? Or if he ask a fish, will he for a fish give him a serpent? Or if he shall ask an egg, will he offer him a scorpion? If ye then, being evil, know how to give good gifts unto your children: *how much more shall your heavenly Father give the Holy Spirit to them that ask Him?*"

If you are asking anything of the Father whether through the natural or in the Spirit, He is not going to give you something evil in return. He will give us better things than our natural fathers could ever give us. So be at ease when it comes to praying in the Spirit and having no understanding of what you're saying. Remember, it's encrypted and only the Father can interpret it.

In Romans 8:26, the Apostle Paul shares another truth about praying in the Spirit,

> "Likewise the Spirit also helpeth our infirmities: for we know not what we should pray for as we ought: but the Spirit itself maketh intercession for us with groanings which cannot be uttered."

We are told in this verse (and in verse 23) by the Apostle Paul that our spirit GROANS within. We groan within because:

1. _____
2. _____

We are told that the Holy Spirit, who is in us, helps our infirmities (weaknesses). This word "weaknesses" is the NT Greek *astheneia* which means "an inability to produce results." From this definition, what are some of the weaknesses that you may have that you need the Holy Spirit to help you with?

_____
_____
_____
_____

What does the Holy Spirit do in order to help us in our weaknesses?

_____

_____

_____

How do we know when the Holy Spirit is interceding for us?

_____

_____

_____

According to Romans 8:28, 29, what benefits do we gain from the intercession of the Holy Spirit?

1. Romans 8:28 _____

2. Romans 8:29 _____

Building Your Prayer Life
Let's Begin to Pray!

Now that you have read the book and have the end of the workbook, it is time to put your training on prayer into practice; it's time to begin building your powerful prayer life. One of the best ways to begin prayer is by the usage of a "prayer list." Let's build our prayer list from the Lord's Prayer that we've learned:

Tell God who He is and what He means to you. "Lord you are …"

_____
_____
_____
_____

Pray according to His will: "Lord let your kingdom come and your will be done …" What are some specific things that God has instructed you to do? (He may have used your pastor, your spouse or someone else to speak a confirming word to you – that is lined up with Scripture)

_____
_____
_____
_____

"Give us this day our daily bread." List your needs and pray for God to fulfill them.

_____
_____
_____
_____
_____

"Forgive us our debt as we forgive our debtors." What are some sins, both inward and outward, sins of commission and omission, which you want to ask God to forgive you for. And list the people who may have hurt you and forgive them.

_____
_____
_____
_____
_____
_____

Prayer of deliverance (from temptation and evil): List some things you are struggling with or troublesome situations you are in that you need God to deliver you from.

_____
_____
_____
_____
_____

"For thine is the kingdom, the power and the glory forever." List the things that you are thankful to God for and tell God what He means to you (show Him some passionate adoration).

_____
_____
_____
_____
_____

Once you have written down your list of specific prayer points, begin to audibly verbalize and say them aloud. This is your prayer to God. Don't think it is wrong to pray this prayer every day until you see God's answer. Jesus said in Luke 11:9, 10,

> "Ask, and it shall be given; seek, and ye shall find; knock, and it shall be opened unto you. For every one that asketh receiveth; and he that seeketh findeth; and to him that knocketh it shall be opened."

PRAY UNTIL YOU GET RESULTS!

One final note: your prayer list will often change because of new trials you experience, different needs to be met, different sins that you may commit and need to confess, new assignments from God to fulfill, and most of all because GOD WILL ANSWER your requests that you put before Him.

www.ingramcontent.com/pod-product-compliance
Lightning Source LLC
Chambersburg PA
CBHW081339080526
44588CB00017B/2685